FIELDS OF FO

by Robin Fulton

Instances (1967)
Inventories (1969)
The Spaces Between the Stones (1971)
The Man with the Surbahar (1971)
Tree-Lines (1974)
Selected Poems 1963–1978 (1980)

Robin Fulton

Fields of Focus

Anvil Press Poetry

Published in 1982
by Anvil Press Poetry Ltd
69 King George Street London SE10 8PX
ISBN 0 85646 081 8

Printed in Hungary

This book is published
with financial assistance from
The Arts Council of Great Britain

ACKNOWLEDGEMENTS

Nearly all of the poems collected here have appeared
individually and acknowledgements are due to: The
Arts Council, *Aquarius*, B.B.C. Radio 3, *Brunton's
Miscellany*, *Encounter*, *Honest Ulsterman*, *The Hudson
Review*, Interim Press, *Lines Review*, *Malahat Review*,
Megaphone, *New England Review*, *New Statesman*, *Oasis*,
Outposts, P.E.N., *Planet*, *Poetry* (Chicago), *The Poetry
Review*, *The Scotsman*, *Scottish Poetry Eight* and *Nine*,
and *The Times Literary Supplement*.
   The poems here are printed in the order in which they
were written: their dates range from 1973 to 1979.
Selected Poems 1963–1978 (Macdonald Publishers,
Loanhead, 1980) draws on five previous
collections and includes a final section of poems
from the 1970s, but none of the latter are duplicated
here.

Contents

Passing Events

Spring: behind us evenings quietly open,
spaces between houses and trees dilate.

I see an old newspaper in a corner:
it's full of hard facts that have softened and dried
hard again after weeks of change.

Suddenly it makes a dash across
open ground scaring a pigeon up –
then lies deceptive as a jumping-jack
whose lit fuse seems to have failed.
I keep an eye on it till I'm out of range.

As the days widen I notice
I'm walking further just to get home.

In Touch

Everyone's setting out in the mist. Paris
is in a cloud somewhere: the plane knows.
I take a night-train west.
      Dawn.
Hour after hour of birch-boles in the mist
like the white sticks of a blind population.
A notice saying CHARLOTTENBURG is the first
clear message, in letters so huge
only the blind could fail to read them. We cross
an invisible border and the train pauses.

A virtuoso blackbird – he's like
a pianist playing alone in an empty hall.

The forest continues.
My memory has retreated to my fingertips.

Outlook

At last the clear view I've had
all winter is closed.

The trees are no longer ghosts
flaunting their transparency
but now fill out with green
and stand like broad conspirators
between me and what I've seen.

The eye is not merciful.
It reads your face like a sheet of braille
but won't rest there: it sees
always beyond your shoulder
inhuman distances.

I cultivate its weakness,
send it into the wanton traps
of a flowering cherry branch and watch
a world and its after-images blur:
I count out each minute by touch.

Museums and Journeys

An exhibition: a hundred years of Edinburgh life.
Coming out I move as heavily as a diver
on the ocean floor: one step, one breath
against the weight of the invisible dead. So many
yet the air is clear. And they've no time for me,
their view of the future blocked by giant headlines.

A journey: one I didn't want to take but took
shutting my eyes – a child again hoping the needle
wouldn't hurt. Lakes and forests, lakes and forests
pass with the weightless ease of delirium. So many.
My view of the past stays clear but hard to read
like a radio-map of a secret corner in the night sky.

Museums and journeys. We meet as strangers do
at the end of long ellipses over continents.
We exchange histories. Our view of the present is clear
but the landscapes go on sliding past. So many
memories, I try to say 'One at a time!'
They keep piling up like urgent unanswered letters.

Remembering Whitsun

Each tree, each room in the house has its own voice:
like a blind man I can orientate myself listening
to wind in leaves, invisible hands ruffling aspens.
Here I am at the phone, my voice instantly
surviving forests without distortion.

Here I am remembering Whitsun years
back, putting the phone down, listening to
silence snapping shut along the length of the wire.

Frontiers

'I used to stand at the frontiers of my senses
like a customs official paid to look suspicious!'
Those confessions. In the pale summer dark
I meet a tall pine still in his prime
though his branches are not in perfect order:
he's still on duty, but perhaps past caring
having watched too many people like me
plundering into the forest with delicate retinae.

I pause and look suspiciously at him.
I don't confuse myself and the lenient fir.
No objection. The forest swallows me up.

Midsummer Nights

Past midnight, the sky already white:
soft clouds can't stop, pines
sway from the waist, aspens hiss.

                              My house
when at last I reach it looks at me
with the pallor of someone close to death.
I must sleep, I fumble with dark blinds,
imagine the walls going transparent,
mutter *if only the mirrors could be black.*

You Occupy My Dreams

You occupy my dreams, casually enter
and leave the rooms of a familiar house,
you and you I forgot to photograph:
dreams focus sharp but can't hold.
(The prints I have I prefer not to see.)

The house dissolves, I have a sixth sense
of the endless miles around me I can't see,
every direction's open, I'm free to move.
But I stand locked in by the very air,
I have become my own fixed image.

'Thank you for the past, I'll lock it up.'
You open a door which I know isn't there.
You wave goodbye. Your logic terrifies.
Waking: 'in this absolute dark
how can you find your way away from me?'

Revelations

Like a huge eye: an intolerable flash
of pure vision, then a roar of pain.
A whole day's light compressed in a second

and the landscape 'as it really is' – leaves
in X-ray, animals' brains at ebb,
our skulls nestling in haloes of imagination.

In light or dark, for us the clichés are real:
the hair I don't have on my spine rises,
at the window the dead faces jump into life.

The TV at least is blank, switched off.
All evening it was a cool polyglot.
The dead and the living faces stared through me

even the frantic woman on the smuggled film
blackening and flashing because of the 'bad conditions'
as she listed her husband's sufferings 'under treatment',

the banal delirium of facts 'as they really are',
fact upon fact, her Russian so feverish
the Swedish subtitles could hardly keep up.

I count seconds. Continuous replay.
The first crackle of rain is the sudden clattering
of a terrified crowd in a narrow street.

A Tree Alone

What is so strange about a tree alone in an open field?'
You never really answered. And I never insist.

I took a journey alone, came back alone, and the tree
had spent all day standing alone in the mist.

(The mist cleared once and in a field I saw
a horse lying sleeping. Or it could have been dead.)

And late into the night I spelt my way like a child
through proof-sheets of old poems, my red

marks like warnings: 'Deceased – Not To Be Disturbed.'
But I keep rising, promisingly alive, although

the moment I recognise me I keep turning away
into a future I scarcely expect *me* to know.

Moonlight. Clarity at last. The tree gleams by itself.
I feel secure making certain he's still there

but I don't ask close questions of my doppelgänger.
By the look in his eyes he doesn't seem to know I'm here.

The Waiting-Room

I sit thinking of a rowing-boat I saw
at rest on transparent water, not
quite at rest, testing its rope, testing
the weight that kept it steady and weightless.

Something from Beethoven goes on and on
at the side of my mind, like a bad-tempered neighbour.
Strange how so much impatience
won through to such inhuman calm.

I wait. A fan drones away. It's so
monotonous the room could be in flight.
I sit staring at a mirror. All it shows
is the reflection of a pale barred window.

Travelling North in Spring

A place whose name means 'middle of the wood'.
Then, a town Germans once razed.
And on. Each place, distorting like
the notes of the crossing-bells, lets us through.

Things take their revenge on the naked eye.
White birches, yellow wooden houses
incandesce. I close my eyes – the snow
burns through, someone is demanding an answer.
I try to concentrate on a basking log
forgotten with a mile of blue water to itself.
No use. It's past. Lean torrents
explode down unscaleable rocks.

Spring gets later. At journey's end I try
to imagine dark woods. I find myself
looking up at a saint with a sword in his hand.
The pavement gives more light than it receives.

To Friends Who Crossed a Frontier

The shelves are warped with books sent from home.
We sit talking. All the clear day
I seemed to have long vision. Now your faces
loom beside me in wide-screen close-up.

Music too. It seeps from the other side,
softens new foundations, 'not in the interest'
of the new life. Pictures of the worn city
fingered over like photos of a dead child.

Two people in one, and one forbidden.
A non-person has such a vivid life.
'The river's dirty, at night it's beautiful.'
The new language closes in like mist.

Home Thoughts

If I were to return now after
'an absence'? But while absent I have gained
too much presence. It's where I live.

I add years, change houses, keep
track of myself. I post letters to the past
and answers come, always up to date.

The generations are always catching up.
The tall historic houses will still be leaning
forward like runners waiting for the starting-gun.

It's dusk – but for a pin-hole in the clouds:
a ray of sunlight glares on an empty field.
Something I can't see is being interrogated.

Decades

I watch three men cutting a hedge away.
Slowly the space between the houses widens out
and the grey October morning goes on filling it.

Something I can't see opens, I step in.

I watch them spreading piles of new white gravel
and when at last their circling crunching footsteps leave
something I can't see quietly opens again

and again I step in, still see nothing.

Perhaps something I saw in the thirties and can't remember
refuses to be forgotten. It lies at the back of my mind
like a forgotten prism catching the occasional light.

I let it be, step back and watch today.

Time for the news. A famous violinist has died:
a little music in the space between world events
and newly dead hands seem to be playing again.

I switch the world off. It's gone. Outside

autumn's at full thrust. On the newly exposed lawn
pale weathered light seeps out of the mist
onto dozens of big brown leaves like lost gloves.

One Hour into a New Year

I drive past the zoo. Not a light.
All those peculiar brains asleep.
Small images must still flicker
from homes on drifting continents.
I drive past the hospital. It's dimmed.
All those exiles planted beyond
their own horizon, still in sight of home.
I wait at red lights where no one crosses
and drive past a house where friends lived.
All gone. Oceans between us now.
Their faces like Victorian photos stare
through me. Move once and I'll recognise.

Not Far from the Beginning

Just three weeks past the shortest day
and already mid-afternoons are whiter,
streets broader. The sun's gone but the snow gives
off daylight like a late sky in midsummer.
Everything echoes. I keep thinking of open spaces

like the first few metres of a long journey: we move
slowly beyond the range of voices on dark water,
we watch the lights huddle and suddenly they're not there
and it's cold on deck, we hurry in and watch our coffee
keeping its head level on a tilting continent.

Walking on ice we concentrate on our feet. We still
feel we could reach out and touch the old year.
Offices switch off, but the buildings don't vanish
at once, they hover, still visible, death-masks.
Sounding like breaking glass, cars edge homewards.

Listening to Rachmaninov in a New House

A storm on the building-site. It's un-shipshape,
plastic sheeting in a frenzy to shred itself free.
And outside my window raw pale boulders
clawed up – from how many dark ages?

But each roof is tested, ettless to holding fast.
I fingerprint fresh timber, like touching a branch
far into the forest: anonymous perhaps
yet the memory-cells in my fingertips keep it.

There's so much space in the present. My letters travel
like solitary migrating birds, they find the address,
but small spaces between words can be so wide
years can slip through, ring after ring in the tree.

A resinous house then with no smell of the past.
The dead wood will live through generations
not mine. At night I listen to the forest in my head
and christen the new house with music written in exile.

Stopping by Shadows

High up, birches have a homely aspect,
small, like things we discover and recognise,
returning after an absence of many years.
Closer, they're almost transparent in the snow
and above, boulders big as cathedrals poise
– on the edge since prehistory.

Midday. I stop at the edge of the shadow
that has filled this space all winter,
the sun a white breath at the cliff-top,
a brief flame in the ice of a remote tree.
I turn and watch my own shadow dissolving
slowly in the luminous dark air

then take a cold step back to life,
skis hiss-hiss on snow-crystals
that spent all night quietly hardening.
Across the valley red and yellow figures
on a brilliant field jump into focus
like true events under a microscope.

Resolutions

All day the air got harder and harder.
I woke in the small hours, rooftops

frozen seas of tranquillity, while far
below the first flakes fell on the street.

The air of another planet come down to earth,
we breathe harshly between familiar stones.

No place for flesh. Spirit and bone
at odds, the nerves caught between, singing:

'Must it be?' It must be must be must be
bouncing like a ball in a small room without windows.

Birthdays

You want to hide. You say it's like
a taxi ride in a foreign city,
when'll it end? – panic and price
and blood-pressure and a lost address.

Perhaps. I think of forests,
an apparition not stark
but like the slow freshening
of a birch among dark surrounding conifers.

Coming Back

I forget the sea, passing the first
lighthouse after a voyage.
I drive home through forests,
darkness rising between pines.

New memories fold for the night.
The forest goes on growing in the dark
where I lie thinking of the slow rings
behind me, around me, before me.

Light from the North

My watch could well be a century out.
I walk past birch-boles, they're pale
like the dark side of the moon clear at last.

My hand rests on a smoothed pine plank
whose years flow like thin lines of water
from a calm boat. The forest is best

now, wide day at dead of night,
I feel like someone wakened from an illness
still knowing how far he's been.

I look towards morning but it's yet
white and cold like the lake through trees.
I wait for sleep, as horizontal as I can.

Something Like a Sky

Something in us has suddenly cleared.
Like a sky.
Like a still-life, alive.
Behind us, our footsteps and voices.
Beyond the walls, a wide silence.
The air is white and open, ready for snow.

High Thoughts

The sun's *always* there. Hard for us
cloud-watchers to believe something lasts.
But high enough it's true: we can leave
earth quite out of sight and mind,
most in our element out of it,
always surprise at light on a tilting wing.

Last night I paused by the library,
cloud-shadows flowing on the glass walls
behind which centuries of thoughts
wait, always there, the elegant
confused cries, 'It's me!'
And each book dumb as an old photograph.

Haunts

I am my own sufficient ghost. I hatch
catastrophe after catastrophe
as the evening tangles, at last lie
intent on the nest of silence I imagine
in an empty room in an empty house in a storm,
deep-breathing away my shallow terrors

only to crawl through dream tunnels
not knowing they are dreams. I find
a way from one labyrinth to the next
with a dazed assurance that would win prizes
in daylight though what occurs here
would not in daylight do me credit.

Morning. I drive through spring snow,
flakes bg as hands, all opaque.
Another dimension seeping through to ours –
am I thankful enough that I can't see,
that aps in the air are not transparent?
The street happens to me and the day follows.

Ancient Timber

The roof *restored* in the 1490s . . . carved
bears still clutching their staffs, power
we admire briefly, preferring to pause longer
by old houses that have spent centuries
twisting into the shape of trees again.
Something in the dead wood refuses to die.

Night. On the way home we briefly admire
a giant constellation atilt and faint
above cherry blossom like carved stone.
Given time (more than we've got)
we could watch the Great Bear dissolve.
Given time, nothing constellates.

But we do, for a time. Our rich hours
lightly weigh into our instant past.
We can hold each other round the clock
and still ask: is skin-deep deep?
Beyond touch, where do we find each other?
Something between us refuses to let go.

Something We Didn't Know Was There

Goldfish in the reflection of bricks.
The steep buildings round us, barely a glimpse
of English perspectives beyond,
moderate hills, moderate groups of trees,
the steep buildings murmur like transformers,
all the words we don't hear, the eyes
we don't see, the work we are not doing.

I seem to start dreaming. Landscapes
small and distant, close-by and large,
grow dull. We could be trapped in a faded
photograph a hundred years old,
figures beyond remembrance or pity,
less recognisable than things,
ageless grass seeding in clear focus.

Dreams chill. And sounds. In the quiet
bushes sparrows are chirping louder and louder.
The pond wrinkles and grows young again
and wrinkles. We shiver at last and look up –
eclipse! A black hole where the sun should be.
We believe what we see, we believe
extremes when we see them and hurriedly gather

books, coats, ask 'Are you cold?'

Hot Days in Cambridge

'King's Closed.' No chance to see
stone mimicking air. No matter –
the act will still be there lives from now.

Instead, we row in circles on heavy water
and ask how many pages are in a tree
and trudge round on deserts that were lawns

and listen to the languages of Europe
strain and wilt, tired defenceless wings.
We all wait for evening, and evening comes

bringing Haydn's *Creation* on the radio,
music from an unheard-of future
when these stones were sweated into place.

Our bodies radiate, they're winter stoves.
All night beside an open window
cool air is iron on my wet back.

Night Alone

Friends, you walk away beneath trees
you've known since childhood. On dark earth
you walk like brief gentle visitors.
We call goodnight earnestly as if
morning will be another continent
and none of us will know the word for 'morning'.

One of me, the one who talks and waves, ·
turns a switch and lets the darkness in
and falls asleep at ease in the forest silence.
The forest is never silent. My other me,
the stubborn one who never talks and can't
lies awake as always listening listening

to sounds behind sounds as night opens
outwards and down. How deep and far
does silence lie? Nothing there to stare
out. He gropes, switches music on,
music that falls like light across his body,
that continent without words for anything.

Notes for a Summer

The Seasons we can always play again.
Our summer's ended, new prints
we can copy and send, copy and send.
Outside: leaves dead from drought.
Inside: music imitating rain.

'Our' summer? We passed a graveyard
and I thought of heavy stacked photo-plates,
pictures waiting undeveloped, water
and calm trees invisible and black.
Tomorrow grows wider and wider, waiting.

Vivaldi clicks off. Silence. Back
to spring again? No. Sleep. And the first
few slow inches of a long journey.

Travelling

Islands crawl across the wet windows.
They swell, undulate in slow motion,
shrivel astern, keep looming past
as sky and water blacken into night.

We step ashore, keeping our own size
while the boat-lights shrink and disappear
and the island grows wide around us.
We breathe raw earth and potato haulms.

We draw blinds. The room's secure now.
It's bigger than the island. And the wind
so loud and near in withered rowans
still keeps a certain quiet distance

as we spread worn maps under the lamp
and remind each other of where we've been.
At last, behind closed eyelids
nothing holds us in, we drift out.

Next morning I look down from a plane
on glittering blue water, punctual boats
on tiny endless voyages to and fro
between placid immovable islands.

Night-Travelling

A juniper, ice and slate-
grey berries on bowed sprigs
dour green needles, a bright
yellow slash of split branch,
all as dark as the tight roots.
All the pale colours at rest
within the dark ones, pale
blue in dark blue, white
in black, and the tiny brains
of winter animals asleep.

I guess. Up here it's bright,
no other world to know,
until a message comes saying
'Snow-clearing on runway, hold
for ten minutes.' Hold? Here?
Hang onto thin air?
We bank. The moon rolls under
a wing, pale and harmless,
another world in view at least,
it rolls again, again, agan.

Orbiting to keep still.
Until the spell gets clearance
to break and we're back on a straight
fast line down to the thump
on the wet well-lit earth.
And out. Humped by a heavy bag
my shadow turns left, right,
seems to know the way and I
follow meekly to a room
and close four walls round me.

Coming Down into the First of Winter

Forty minutes will do to change seasons,
white sunlight washing over slabs
of cloud. How long could I stay here,
all of earth hidden? Long enough
to ask, at least, before the cloud softens,
foams, darkens, and I know nothing
except harsh breath and the moan of trams.
It's Edinburgh in 1948
and it's Oslo in 1976.
I check my watch compulsively but it
has a one-track mind – it's today! it's today!

Shrunk snow in the park is ridged like spines.
Fresh flakes crowd past lights,
night without stars, voices, steps.
I look at each flake and always another
as if each one were the first and last.
How long could I stay here in the warm
silence of the snowy streets? I jerk with cold.
Tomorrow, I say, I'll buy a map of the sky.
Tomorrow, I say, I'll fly back to autumn,
berries still piled on leafless rowans.
Tomorrow, I say, as if I'd forgotten something.

Marazion

The Mount – it's so familiar I don't
even say 'There it is at last.'
It is. A postcard true to life.

We're out of season so the beach is bare,
a few waders picking over dull
hanks of weed that just may surprise.
The tide has turned. We could wait and walk
right over, touch it. But don't.

It's how we see our other lives, the ones
we didn't, can't live. We recognise,
move on, know they're still there.

Walking on Snow

A single lamp-post, a mile of dark north
and south. Alone. Improbable.
The home of a soul giving without ever receiving.
All night no one looks at the shining rock.

I folded away *The Night Sky* like a village map.
So many. I saw only one, the first, bright,
tracking across my clear window as if it had
absolute right of way. I stepped out –

leaving stacked words gone silent, in place,
they'd wait for ever if need be then flurry
like snow-flakes in someone else's brain. I smiled
thinking of white paper that would never be written on

and hurried across white earth, the black sky
now crowding with the other stars where they'd been
all day, not noticeably changed.
For five minutes I wish them all still 'fixed'

then look back along my prints in the snow
– they're anonymous already, neatly frozen
for the night, one track among many.
In twelve hours the pale lamp will switch off.

Elegies

The hotel room is cramped, with five
very unequal sides.
I remember first snow
shrinking in grey ordered heaps,
last leaves bright as lemons.
That's Oslo, that's today,
cool oaks and warm stones
we leant against yesterday.
How uncertain – perhaps
I read of this in Mandeville.

I dream of Tresco, raw
mist uncoiling through
un-English palms while we
lose our way on a small
well-mapped island.
That's true as well. Waking
I add: through a bright chasm
the helicopter pounced at last.
If seeing's believing I have
summer stacked on photographs.

I dream again, trapped in
the staves of impossible music,
rigid as concrete,
I don't see but I believe
until I'm back in my narrow room
and wait. Given time and space
all those moments settle.
I think of gentle animals
at ease. They don't mind our presence,
don't seem to notice our absence.

At This Moment

Thinking of friends in several cities,
I know which corners to turn
remember the set of chair and table
hear each voice coming
from room to room: memories
perhaps but in the present tense.

I watch the light go down
yellowing into night, touching
roofs and pinnacles across Europe
right now, at this angle.
Touching too a green field
I once saw from the air:

medieval ditches, lines
of walls, houses, barns, church,
confines of lived lives,
all quite unsettled
now. You could walk across
this field and see nothing.

But from the air it looked like
a picture slowly changed by the eyes
of generations looking at it.

Keeping Steady

Water-borne I watch the boat's shadow
flow over lichen-covered rock,
shadow on shadow as if the lichen
too were on its slow way past.

Air-borne I watch mottled islands
drift with the ease of clouds. I've left
days of my life on one of them and now
I carry the island, an invisible weight.

On land again, still seeing the curved
earth I lean to stay upright
then settle my newest memories
on an old point of balance. It's like the pause
clock-hands make at midnight.

What to Do with the Word 'Home'?

I handle it like an antique-
collector (though I'm none)
back with a prize, unique to him
but heavy, heavier as he stands
at a loss where to set it down.

Would it suit here? Would eight
years of youth qualify?
Bog-myrtle and peewit,
curlew and cotton-grass
are sweet ghosts but don't claim
special attention and don't get it.

The moor's ambiguous. I've no
talent or desire to join
an inch of life lying low
over the spongiest, most
patient of collectors. It is
experienced in swallowing homes.

Can I settle here only
on first arrival, in my pocket
a ticket for the clear sky?
The people who still live here
– they've been moving as fast as I.

A Night and a Morning

Passing the cathedral spire
I see two clock-faces,
one bright, one blank.
How many bricks,
used-up muscles, time
kept like a cold monument.

The library walls are baclk.
Light from a hurrying half-moon
glints on them like seawater.
How many books,
used-up voices, pages
unreadable in the dark.

Almost asleep I turn and see
through a thin drawn curtain
bright windows and road-lights
the height and depth of the hillside.
They're like a dense constellation
less than a hundred years old.

Almost awake again, I think
the white spring light is snow
on roofs and streets. It's not. I try
to focus on an unfamiliar day,
all the dead ones at my back
crowding to watch the new one.

Harpsichord and Plane

Silence before music. I listen to
wooden walls, each creak a slight
adjustment to heat or cold or wind.
The music passes well, colour and scent
of resin, cadences of slow rings.

But how old. I panic at the time
it took from living hand to living ear.
I stare at a lonely house in a picture,
watch the inches round it grow to miles,
someone's life-span circumscribed.

A plane takes off, total noise
all in the present tense, but not for long –
weight becomes grace and noise is spent,
the plane shrinks and disappears into
a future that will last an hour. The fugue

audible again is still growing
the way trees do, despite events.
The shrinking house shrinks, is still there.
If I don't move, I can watch my shadow
inch across decades in the grain.

The Last Moths

Wet birch-boles ripple in my headlights
one by one for miles, behind them miles
of autumn's every red and yellow, more than all
conceived shades, invisible in the dark.

That night I dream of accidents and waken.
I try hard to imagine unconsciousness
but can't. I watch the telephone's silhouette,
it's like the head of an animal asleep, alert.

The last moths of the season have landed on the big
black window, pale undersides to the light.

Hotel Room, New Year

How many have paid, will pay, to lie
in this cube of darkness? I'm one of them.
I ought to consider the dead year but it's still
alive, all those doors I walked through,
now and not-now, landings on solid earth.
Three floors down, music and dancing:
all that reaches me is a manic bass-line
vibrating through walls. There must be a tune,
a loud one, inaudible to me.

Between flights again. Yesterday I watched
from Aberdeen to London all in a slow hour.
Small places that trapped lives, my lordly eyes
skim over, geography come alive,
so more-than-life-size it's hard to think
people inhabit it. Passing over cloud
I try: windscreen wipers fail to clear
mist, new cancer patients fail to waken
from a nightmare that won't stop.

My too-heavy case is ready to weigh me down
again tomorrow. I listen for a sign of change,
one door opening, one door closing.
My seventh sense hears it but says nothing to me.
All I hear when the walls quieten is
a kind of forest silence over the crowded roofs.
I expect to hear a cone drop miles away
at my side. It must be past midnight.
I must already be locked inside another year.

East Coast Revisited

Johnshaven, that was three years.
Edinburgh, that was thirteen.
Holy Isle, that was two visits
with fifteen years between them.

Is this being god-like, watching
autobiography at a safe height?
The cabin is full of sunlight; folded
papers carry sensations from earth.

Less god-like to chafe at not
moving from the spot for a day or more;
eyes learning to store horizons;
wearing my watch all night, a fixed star.

From 1939

What quick hands the dead have, and eyes
more metallic than a blackbird's.
I'm alive, but slow, and so much
has happened since, I listen to him play
through a noise like early rain on leaves.

On an Etching of Dedham Vale
by Glynn Thomas

A rural *mappamundi*, stream and stile,
random English fields become a world
in a fish-eye lens, and at the centre
convolvulus and poppy, man-size.

A world to carry through the world, a check
on the eye's life-long growing pains.
Lesson One is 'Take your time!'
Lesson Two: 'Your time is running out!'

Time I spend in 'Dedham Vale' is time
that waits, with interest, behind the glass.

Following a Mirror

I look past a stranger's eyes and see,
out through an open door, a line
of leafless birches like blind men
leading west. The mirror can't stop:
an ocean, white ruins of icebergs,
a prairie, parallels converging,
a desert, towns with pale street-grids
and invisible houses, El Paso
down through the hazed skyline.
The mirror keeps everything I lose.

I sleep. The mirror stays awake in the dark.
The stranger's eyes are shut. The mirror hurries
surefooted on narrow cliff paths,
its memory for local history
immaculate, how to find houses –
one of Caithness flags with a deep press
stacked with nineteenth-century boxes;
a manse in Arran, prewar rain
smudging garden trees; last year's
hotel room, a slit view of the Cam. . .

And all crowded. People I forgot
and those I remember exchange faces.
Sharp details swell like thunder clouds,
meeting-rooms grow minuscule.
Trapped in a rib-cage, I stop breathing

gasp at the last moment, break into
morning – morning, a place I didn't choose,
a wide hall where I wait for baggage
while out on wet tarmac behind me
engines that have droned all night cool.

Loss of Outlook

Easter. Days with no workmen
hammering up moulds, pouring soft
concrete, waiting, undoing wood.
No walls will rise today. The sky
is heavy as old snow. New snow
rots to a clockwork drip round
the clock from half-finished thresholds.
Through wet glass I watch high
wet gallows lean in the east wind.

I think of midwinter when I watched
fresh snow pile on timber stacked
beside a measured square cut in rock.
My westward view of trees was still clear.
Smell of snow on smell of cut pine.
And five wrens went bounce bounce
between piled stack and piled eave
while a red sun went right down
and wouldn't come again for eighteen hours.

By midsummer my view will be gone.
So will the tall crane whose double chain
sways all night with empty hands.
Wood will be stacked to rise again
on other sites. Windows come for those
about to acquire newer and higher views
than the one I thought worth keeping.
I'll see a wall beyond which light
clouds and planes with rows of people fly.

Spring Light

Another day of relentless. . . not heat
but cold inspectorial light.

Sky and earth have both widened out –
a millimetre perhaps but enough
to stretch spaces between stones, trees,
houses. The light will brook no shade:
holds out like bad workmanship
slices of rock, building-site slag,
collapsed barns. 'Nothing will grow here!'
Rejected spots muffled in kinder times
by leaves or snow are open now to a gaze
that finds too many too bad.

Taking longer and faster strides I need
more of them to cover my measured walk.
I feel like a tightened membrane. What
ear-splitting whisper may crack?

Not till evening the sky's hold gives.
A stain north-westwards into red.
Stones, trees, houses close in,
spaces between them fertile, full.
I pause at a spatter of black buds against
high metallic blue. Beside me, lopped
maple and lopped pine gauchely hold
up stumps that will never cure.
I turn to the evening star – long lost
familiar, kind childhood lamp,

but he too is hectic marking time.
His one sharp eye sees me home.

Hurrying in Spring

An ambulance makes a straight white line through
twisting traffic corners. It hoots and wails in dis-
cordant keys. Inside someone stoops.

In a wet country a week without rain is drought.
Avenue pines have grey undersides.
Rude spirals of dust dervish at crossing-places.

Spring is nervous. Or I am. I seem to stride
on a moving walkway, walls rush with ease.
Calm days I try to think of all shake
together, slip, their vertical hold awry.
Something in me's like a compass-needle that knows
where north is but can't, for trembling, rest and point.

Passing Verdun

Some things ought to be looked at
even if they're no longer there.
At last I'm near enough to see which
gentle slopes were worth such pain.
I'm driving east from Rheims. The closer I get,
the tighter the autobahn's grip on me.
Signs I've waited for point, I can't
obey, I'm on rails, I'm carried past. . .

I cross a border, turn north, stop
at a house with thick walls and echoing rooms.
I wind my watch back and gain an hour.
The hour darkens like an old photograph
till I can see Cassiopeia, stars
so slow they were once called fixed.
Headlights float in pairs round
a wood-edge, short-lived as moths.

I fell asleep that night locked
as a kernel in a hard shell of silence.

Waking in Jylland

Under this Danish heath do more
acrid survivors wait to be raised?

I waken to a harsh sun, a glare through
thin curtains, an undipped headlight.
Last night's moon haunting us
between clouds was like glints of truth.

In my dream the rendezvous was a rock
whose steep sides were incurably smooth.
I couldn't see how my son could climb.
He couldn't see how I couldn't.

Tonight the clouds will be complete. We'll give
up hopes of seeing the moon's eclipse
and drive till daylight through a race
of private souls sunk in their own events,

through a language remembered now only
in lit rooms by night-shift workers.

Note for a Japanese Poet

'Hitomaro.' Something lands softly
on the net of my feelings. At first I don't
think of the thirteen centuries,
our instant panic if we met.
'I can't. . .'
is what we'd each say, fail to say,
forgetting to look up at the twisting elms
that had already made him make sense to me.

Listening to a Curlew

1

A perpetual silence at my side.
Everything I hear leans
towards it, like trees stooped
by a lifetime's coastal wind.
Or in the deep rock beneath
our feet seams rise and dip
we'll never see. Or at a play
we step on layers we didn't know
were there, they give, they hold, they give,
and after the last words hands
try to clap the silence away.

2

Me, under a saguaro.
Next, you, instead of me.
We prove what we can – 'July,
'77, Arizona.'
Count woodpecker holes
but not a wing whirrs. Stare
at the thundercloud about to pour
boulders across the desert road.
We couldn't see the next hours
we've now lost. We couldn't hear
this silence that we've saved.

3

We always know what came next.
Listening to the prelude

we always hear the silent fugue.
What comes next – each hour
I follow the glass wall between
the good silence and the bad.
On which side? What will I hear?
On this side I say thanks
be to silences that let,
say, a brief curlew's
voice ring year after year.

A Note from Flevoland

I left Cologne yesterday,
quick distances between
one and many to negotiate,
and thanks to the overcrowding dead
for each next vacant step.
Today I came to Lelystad,
the solidarity of five-
sided stones that won't budge,
blocking the sea off from new
Dutch acres and their unborn.

I think back to where I began,
each passer-by, in dark
thirties clothes, an event.
I think forward to where I live,
space around me slow to fill.
In crowds I nurture a certain moorland
loneliness. Away from them,
hearing footsteps in streets
that aren't there, to left, to right,
I walk steady on my rope of silence.

Finds, *circa* 1948

Lupins. Father-figures. I reached up
and rolled a ball of dew from a green hand.

Calendulas. They made widows older,
curtains paler, afternoons heavier.

Harebells on crumbling grassy cliffs.
My fear of edges became lifelong.

Wild nasturtiums by a pool deeper
than places of silence and perpetual night.

A Photo, A Clock

'May.' The year, I forgot to write.
The hands say ten thirty-three.
They've said so, for decades perhaps?
Long enough, in this red and green
preserved clock-maker's house. Round
the giant dial thirty-two points
make it a sun, a cogged wheel in some
heavenly device. And you paused
a nervous five-hundredth of a second,
clear as frost
beside a stopped clock whose hands are blurred
and watery beyond your field of focus.

Revisiting a Clock

September rushed. It stopped only when we
stopped, again, in front of the stopped clock.
That fits. This is the 'old' town,
a genuine dead street in dead Aarhus.
Through-traffic for visitors: at night
any visitants will not be seen.
I take another picture but the glass
between me and the burnished spiked dial
is too alive,
thronged with eager shadows. Back to the car
we say, with cold hands and headaches, follow
follow the scurrying white backs of leaves.

Five Moments

The first grows and grows.
Hospital corridors.
I watch 'me' panic.

*

The second only shrinks,
black dwarfish, choked
by its own density.

*

The third brings ease.
Light and silence seep
through a labyrinth.

*

Years I reach across:
still warm, like a glove
just taken off.

*

My death is there. A month,
a day, an hour. It has
the weight of a small leaf.

Reading a Page

I stare at a well-made page. Words
that will never break ranks wait
for me. I hardly reach the first stop,
turning and turning to the window to watch
a generation of snow in thin air,
fluff, soon soft ragged discs,
mass obedience to one law,
identical souls, homonyms. . .
the snow-flakes crowd in. The whiter
the light gets the less there is to see.

The page is black, the words an icicle.
I blow on it, it melts, it melts not,
and someone says: 'This is your page,
you have only one, birth at the top,
death on the bottom line. Each day
survived means more to miss out,
the summary becomes denser, clear truth
defying nature, clearer as it thickens.'
Even my four decades begin
to glow with their own concentration.

Remembering Walls

I once wanted these walls
to turn magically clear
as air and let me walk through.

Now that strangers have moved in
strange furniture I want
the house stone-solid and dour,

resisting the dank strath winds
and to the dry pine-descant
adding a worn ground-bass

angular, melancholy.
It follows me from winter to
winter. Safe in its lulls

voices that cannot last long,
that did not always please me,
will last as long as I shall.

No one watches the wet slates
dry and glisten again and dry.
My private music remembers me.

Walking in Woods

Trees with the patience of sleep-walkers
who've stopped and forget to move on.
Woods have their own gradual timetables.

I move too quickly to catch more
than forest trivia, patiently years
creak, not a hint of a Great Plan.

In part of the timetable I can't see
trees waken and move to the next stance.
They need space, passing circumspectly.

I come home knowing little as ever.
Resin wears off. I almost hear
a music so slow it can't be heard.